TOY STORY

T0351213

Level 2

Re-told by: Gregg Schroeder
Series Editor: Rachel Wilson

Before You Read

In This Book

Woody

Andy

Buzz Lightyear

Activity

Find the page with ...

1 a room ready for a party.
2 some presents.
3 the toys meeting Buzz Lightyear.
4 two toy friends.

This is Woody.

He is Andy's favorite toy and he sits on Andy's bed.

He wears a sheriff's hat and badge.

Andy has some interesting toys.
He plays with them every day.
Some of them are funny animals.

Today is Andy's birthday.
"Happy birthday, Andy!" his mother says.
The room is ready for his party.

Andy's friends arrive and they bring presents.
He's excited.
Does he get a bicycle, a toy plane, or a toy car?

What's this present on Andy's bed?
It's not a car and it's not a plane.
It's a space ranger toy!

SPACE RANGER LIGHTYEAR

The toys are looking at this new toy.
"Hello!" he says. "I'm Buzz Lightyear,
Space Ranger."

Woody is angry. Buzz is on Andy's bed!
"You're a toy!" Woody says.
"No, I'm a space ranger," Buzz answers.

Woody laughs and points at Buzz.
Buzz is a toy, but he doesn't know it!
Woody doesn't like Buzz.

"Okay. What can you do?" Woody asks Buzz.

"Show us!"

"I'm a space ranger and I can fly," Buzz says.

His wings are open.
He jumps on a ball. *BOING!*
Then Buzz is flying high in the room!

Now he's over the bed.
He flies well and he flies fast.

Buzz is back on the bed.
Wow! He's fast! The toys like the space
ranger. They think he's smart.

Woody thinks about Buzz.
He knows Buzz can't fly.
But is that important?

In the end, Woody likes Buzz.
They're Andy's toys and *that's* important.
And now they're good friends!

After You Read

1 **Choose the right answer.**

1 The toys like Buzz. He is *smart* / *dangerous*.
2 Woody is Andy's *new* / *favorite* toy.
3 Buzz can *swim* / *fly*.
4 At the end of the story, Woody and Buzz are *sad* / *happy*.

2 **Read and say Yes or No.**

1 Andy likes Woody.
2 Andy's birthday is today.
3 Buzz is a sheriff.
4 Woody has wings.

3 **Who says this?**

> Buzz   Mom   Woody

1 "Happy birthday, Andy!"
2 "You're a toy!"
3 "I can fly."

Picture Dictionary

badge

birthday party

fast

fly

laugh

plane

presents

smart

wing

Phonics

Say the sounds. Read the words.

F f

face

funny

th

think

teeth

Say the tongue twister.

I think I see a funny face and three thin teeth.
I think I see a funny face and four fat teeth.

Values

Believe in your own abilities.

Find Out

Do you play with old toys or new toys?

All children love toys and games.
Children play with marbles at school.
But do you know? Marble games are very old.

marbles

Very old toys

teddy bear

Old toys

Today, blocks are a favorite toy. Children make things with them.

Some children play with new toys. They play virtual reality games!

blocks

Toys today

virtual reality toy

New toys

Pearson Education Limited
KAO Two
KAO Park, Harlow,
Essex, CM17 9NA, England
and Associated Companies throughout the world.

ISBN: 978-1-2923-4670-0

This edition first published by Pearson Education Ltd 2020

7 9 10 8

Set in Heinemann Roman Special, 19pt/28pt
Printed by Neografia, Slovakia

Published by Pearson Education Limited

Acknowledgments
Alamy Stock Photo: Lucie Lang 20, M.L.Miller 20
Getty Images: aldomurillo/ E+ 18, Halfdark 21, kali9/ E+ 16
Shutterstock.com: GrashAlex 17, Kalmatsuy Tatyana 18, Mikael Damkier 16, RomanR 17, TonyV3112
16, yanikap 21

For a complete list of the titles available in the Pearson English Readers series, visit
www.pearsonenglishreaders.com.

Alternatively, write to your local Pearson Education office or
to Pearson English Readers Marketing Department,
Pearson Education, KAO Two, KAO Park, Harlow, Essex, CM17 9NA